MAR — 2 2021

ELENA DELLE DONNE

Women in Sports

MARY HERTZ SCARBROUGH

Rourke
Educational Media

A Division of
Carson Dellosa Education

Before Reading: *Building Background Knowledge and Vocabulary*

Building background knowledge can help children process new information and build upon what they already know. Before reading a book, it is important to tap into what children already know about the topic. This will help them develop their vocabulary and increase their reading comprehension.

Questions and Activities to Build Background Knowledge:

1. Look at the front cover of the book and read the title. What do you think this book will be about?
2. What do you already know about this topic?
3. Take a book walk and skim the pages. Look at the table of contents, photographs, captions, and bold words. Did these text features give you any information or predictions about what you will read in this book?

Vocabulary: *Vocabulary Is Key to Reading Comprehension*

Use the following directions to prompt a conversation about each word.

- Read the vocabulary words.
- What comes to mind when you see each word?
- What do you think each word means?

> **Vocabulary Words:**
> - burnout
> - cerebral palsy
> - drafted
> - expectations
> - integrates
> - recruit

During Reading: *Reading for Meaning and Understanding*

To achieve deep comprehension of a book, children are encouraged to use close reading strategies. During reading, it is important to have children stop and make connections. These connections result in deeper analysis and understanding of a book.

 Close Reading a Text

During reading, have children stop and talk about the following:

- Any confusing parts
- Any unknown words
- Text to text, text to self, text to world connections
- The main idea in each chapter or heading

Encourage children to use context clues to determine the meaning of any unknown words. These strategies will help children learn to analyze the text more thoroughly as they read.

When you are finished reading this book, turn to the next-to-last page for **After Reading Questions** and an **Activity**.

TABLE OF CONTENTS

BASKETBALL
AND FAMILY

Elena Delle Donne fell in love with basketball when she was four years old. Naturally talented and extremely tall, Elena was on a team with boys three years older than her by second grade. In the final moments of a championship game, Elena's brother passed the ball to her. She made the winning basket.

Elena's close family influenced her childhood. Elena's older sister, Lizzie, is deaf and blind. She also has **cerebral palsy** and autism. The sisters communicate through hugs, touches, and sign language. Elena says Lizzie is her inspiration.

As a teen, Elena volunteered with special needs kids. She majored in special education in college.

cerebral palsy (suh-REE-bruhl PAHL-zee): a disability caused by damage to the brain before, during, or after birth that results in muscular and speech issues

Elena shares her love and knowledge of basketball with Special Olympics athletes.

TRIUMPHS AND CHALLENGES

As a seventh-grader, Elena was offered her first college scholarship. A year later, she was playing with her local high school team and the Delaware All-State team. But Elena wasn't sure she loved basketball. She wondered if maybe she only played because everyone expected it. The thought of leaving Lizzie to play basketball in college also troubled her.

She took one summer off from playing basketball during high school, but Elena kept her doubts to herself. As a sophomore, she averaged 28.5 points per game and made 95 percent of her free throws. She set the girls' high school free throw record and became the top college **recruit** in the United States.

recruit (re-KROOT): a newcomer to a field or activity

Elena accepted a scholarship from the University of Connecticut, a powerhouse in women's basketball. But, she immediately knew she'd made a mistake when she arrived there in June, 2008. She had lost all her passion for basketball, and she couldn't bear being away from Lizzie. She quit after two days. Almost no one understood why.

After leaving Connecticut, Elena spent a lot of time thinking and walking in the woods near her parents' home. At the end of the summer, she decided to go to a nearby school, the University of Delaware. Instead of playing basketball there, she joined the volleyball team. She played joyfully, without the pressure she felt with basketball.

Health Scare

Shortly before starting college, Elena became extremely ill. She was diagnosed with Lyme disease, a bacterial infection. Elena likely got it from a tick bite in the woods. She recovered after being treated with antibiotics.

Elena realized she missed basketball and joined the team in her sophomore year at the University of Delaware. This time, she focused on her love of basketball instead of the **expectations** of others.

Elena's Lyme disease returned. She missed 12 games during her second college season. To get better, she made changes to her lifestyle and diet. She boosted her immune system.

expectations (ek-spek-TAY-shuhns): strong beliefs that something will happen or come true

Throughout college, Elena was determined to avoid **burnout** and play for the love of the sport. She helped her team advance further in tournament play than ever before.

In 2011, Elena played for the U.S. team in the World University Games in China. They won! She developed new leadership skills through the experience.

burnout (BURN-out): an exhaustion of physical or emotional strength or motivation as a result of prolonged stress or frustration

The Chicago Sky **drafted** Elena into the Women's National Basketball Association (WNBA). Named Rookie of the Year in 2013, she averaged 18.1 points per game and made 93 percent in free throws.

Elena even played in the 2016 Olympics. The team won a gold medal, and Elena called it "the most beautiful basketball I've ever played in my life."

drafted (DRAF-ted): selected

Tough Choices

WNBA players are paid only a tiny fraction of the money that men make who play in the National Basketball Association (NBA). Many women boost their income by playing in other countries during the off-season. Elena does not. She spends her time near family.

The year 2017 was great for Elena. She married Amanda Clifton and joined the Washington, DC, Mystics—a team closer to her family. The Mystics made it to the WNBA semifinals in 2017. They lost the final in 2018. Elena helped them win their first-ever WNBA championship title in 2019.

Elena's motto is "*demand excellence.*"

Impressive Stats

- 2015 and 2019 Most Valuable Player (MVP) in the WNBA
- Highest career free throw percentage, male or female (94%)
- Career average 20.28 points per game (second in WNBA)
- 3,853 points in 190 games (2013–2019)

OFF THE COURT

Elena is the author of a series of novels for young readers. It's called *Hoops*. The books feature a six-foot-tall (1.8 meter-tall) basketball-playing seventh-grader named Elle. With a co-author, Elena also wrote a nonfiction book for young adult readers. It's called *My Shot: Balancing It All and Standing Tall*.

Family Support

Elena's family helped put her at ease about her height when she was growing up. But, people could be rude. Once, someone got upset at Elena's mother for allowing an "eight-year-old" to use a pacifier. Elena was three.

Elena is 6 feet, five inches (1.96 meters) tall; the average U.S. woman is about five feet, four inches (1.63 meters) tall.

Elena coaches girls through the De11e Donne Academy basketball camps. She challenges the campers to work hard and make mistakes. She tells them, "that means you're challenging yourself and getting out of your comfort zone."

Elena stresses the importance of having fun and avoiding burnout. She also **integrates** Special Olympics athletes into her camps.

integrates (IN-ti-grates): includes a person or a group into a larger group

Elena has said if she weren't a professional basketball player, she'd be a special education teacher. Here she interacts with Special Olympics athletes from Delaware.

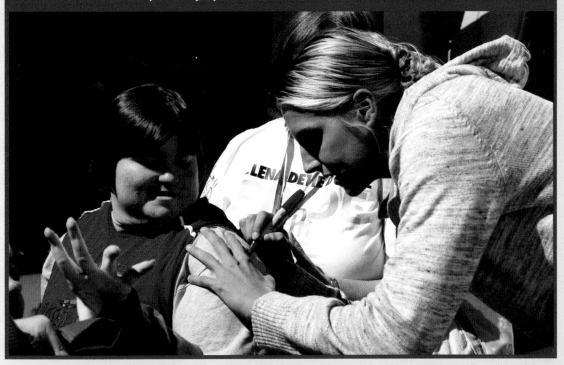

Elena also established the Elena Delle Donne Charitable Foundation to support Lyme disease research and special needs programs. She's a Global Ambassador for the Special Olympics.

Elena and her wife, Amanda, plan to be Lizzie's caretakers eventually. Elena said: "She's never said a word to me, but Lizzie has taught me more than anyone in my life."

Memory Game

Look at the pictures. What do you remember reading on the pages where each image appeared?

Index

Text-Dependent Questions

1. What do you think makes Elena successful and inspiring?

2. What two causes does the Elena Delle Donne Foundation support?

3. Did your understanding of what it takes to be one of the greatest athletes in the world change after reading this book? Explain.

4. What WNBA teams has Elena played for? Which one has won the WNBA Championship?

5. What impact has Lyme disease had on Elena's life?

Activity

Elena established her charitable foundation to raise money and awareness for two causes she's passionate about. If you established a foundation, what would you support? Why? Write a game plan for your future foundation.

About the Author

Mary Hertz Scarbrough loved learning about Elena Delle Donne for this book. She admires Elena's excellence as an athlete and her strong commitment to issues she's passionate about. Mary writes from her home in South Dakota, where she lives with her husband and two rescue dogs. She tries to make the world a better place through volunteer work, advocacy on issues she believes in, and voting in every election.

www.rourkeeducationalmedia.com

Quote sources: Donne, Elena Delle, My Shot: Balancing It All and Standing Tall. 2018 ; Akner-Brodesser, Taffy, "The Audacity of Height," ESPN, November 22, 2016

PHOTO CREDITS: page 4-5: ©Newscom.com; page 6-7: ©ZUMA Wire; page 8-9: ©Shutterstock, ©Scott Grau, Newscom.com; page 10-11: ©Ben Smidt/ Icon Sports Media, Inc. (Icon SMI) ALL RIGHTS RESERVED; page 12-13: ©Shutterstock; page 14-15: ©Shutterstock; page 16-17: ©Shutterstock; page 18-19: ©Newscom.com; page 20-21: ©Newscom.com, ©ZUMA Wire; page 22-23: ©Icon Sportswire (A Division of XML Team Solutions) All Rights Reserved; page 24-25: ©2013 Saquan Stimpson, all rights reserved, ©Represented by ZUMA Press, Inc.; page 27: ©Zuma Wire; page 29: ©Daniel A. Anderson

Edited by: Madison Capitano
Cover and interior design by: Rhea Magaro-Wallace

Library of Congress PCN Data

Elena Delle Donne / Mary Hertz Scarbrough
(Women in Sports)
ISBN 978-1-73163-826-7 (hard cover)
ISBN 978-1-73163-903-5 (soft cover)
ISBN 978-1-73163-980-6 (e-Book)
ISBN 978-1-73164-057-4 (ePub)
Library of Congress Control Number: 2020930240

Rourke Educational Media
Printed in the United States of America
01-1942011937